Dad a

Jackie Tidey

Photographs by Lyz Turner-Clark

Contents

Getting Ready for a Walk

On Saturday,

my dad went for a walk

with his guide dog, Jazz.

Dad likes to walk

by the beach.

First, Dad put on
Jazz's **harness**.

Then they went
out the gate.

Jazz walked
on Dad's left side.

Dad was safe with Jazz.

Crossing the Big Road

They got to a big **road** that they had to cross.

Cars and trucks go very fast along this road.

Jazz stopped walking
at the **traffic lights**.
Dad stopped too.

The green light went
beep, beep, beep!
It was time
for Dad and Jazz to walk.

They walked safely
across the road to the beach.

At the Beach

Dad and Jazz walked along the path by the beach.

Dad cannot see the waves,
but he loves the smell
of the sea.

A big girl was playing
with a dog on the beach.

Jazz did not run after them.
He stayed by my dad.

Home Again

Then it was time for them to go home again.

Dad was happy and safe on his walk to the beach with Jazz.

Glossary

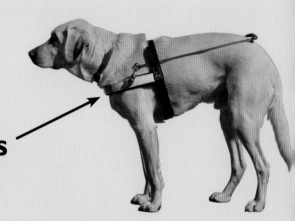

harness

road

traffic lights